Better Homes and Gardens®

PARTY RECIPES

Our seal assures you that every recipe in *Party Recipes*
has been tested in the Better Homes and Gardens® Test Kitchen.
This means that each recipe is practical and reliable,
and meets our high standards of taste appeal.

For years, Better Homes and Gardens® Books has been a leader in publishing cook books. In *Party Recipes,* we've pulled together a delicious collection of recipes from several of our latest best-sellers. These no-fail recipes will make your cooking easier and more enjoyable.

Editor: Rosemary C. Hutchinson
Editorial Project Manager: Rosanne Weber Mattson
Graphic Designer: Harijs Priekulis
Electronic Text Processor: Paula Forest

On the front cover: Golden Glazed Chinese Ribs, Mini Quiches, and Maple-Syrup Appetizers *(see recipes, pages 32 and 33)*

Contents

Tailgate Party

Two bits, four bits, six bits, a dollar! All for a tailgate party, stand up and holler! Tailgate parties and the "big game" go together to create memories of good friends, fun, exciting games, and wonderful food. For your next tailgate party, prepare this easy menu (see recipes, pages 6-9). Your friends are sure to love the out-of-the-ordinary foods.

MENU

Italian Sausages in Brioche
Tailgate Coleslaw *or*
   Italian-Style Pasta Salad
Fresh fruit
Soft drinks or beer

Italian Sausages in Brioche

Pictured on pages 4–5.

1 package active dry yeast ⅓ cup warm water (110° to 115°) ⅓ cup milk ⅓ cup butter *or* margarine ¼ cup sugar ¼ teaspoon salt 3 cups all-purpose flour 2 beaten eggs	● Soften yeast in warm water. In a saucepan heat milk, butter or margarine, sugar, and salt till warm (115° to 120°) and butter is almost melted; stir constantly. Turn into a large mixing bowl. Stir in *1 cup* of the flour; beat well. Add the softened yeast and eggs; stir till smooth. Stir in the remaining flour.
	● Scrape down sides of bowl, forming dough into ball. Cover bowl with plastic wrap. Refrigerate for 2 to 24 hours.
8 links Italian sausage (about 2 pounds)	● Meanwhile, split Italian sausage links lengthwise. Place cut side down, on a rack in a shallow baking pan. Bake, uncovered, in a 350° oven for 25 to 30 minutes or till done. Drain sausages on paper toweling. Let cool about 30 minutes or till nearly room temperature.
3 tablespoons prepared mustard 2 slices cheddar, mozzarella, *or* Swiss cheese	● Spread cut sides of sausages with mustard. Cut cheese into eight 5x¾-inch strips. Place 1 strip on cut side of *8* sausage halves. Top with remaining sausage halves, forming 8 stacks.
1 egg white 1 tablespoon water	● Remove dough from refrigerator. Punch down. Transfer to a lightly floured surface. Divide into 8 equal portions. With floured hands or rolling pin, flatten each into an 8x5-inch oval. Place 1 sausage link on each oval. Wrap dough around sausages, pressing edges to seal. Place seam side down on a greased shallow baking pan. Stir together egg white and water. Brush some egg white mixture atop each. Cover and let rise till nearly double (about 30 to 40 minutes).
	● Bake in a 375° oven for 15 to 18 minutes or till golden. Remove to a wire rack to cool. Wrap tightly and refrigerate. Makes 8 main-dish servings.

MENU COUNTDOWN
1 Day Ahead:
Prepare Italian Sausages in Brioche and refrigerate.
Prepare Tailgate Coleslaw *or* Italian-Style Pasta Salad and refrigerate.
Chill pop or beer.
Pack all nonfood items.
Day of Party:
Pack Italian Sausages in Brioche, Tailgate Coleslaw, *or* Italian-Style Pasta Salad, and pop or beer in cooler.
Pack fresh fruit.

To get rid of excess fat, place the split Italian sausage links, cut side down on a rack in a shallow baking pan.

Place the two halves of the cut Italian sausage links back together, forming a link.

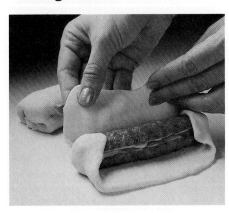

Wrap the brioche dough around the Italian sausage links, pressing the edges of the dough to seal.

Planning a Tailgate Party

It doesn't take hard work, just a little careful planning, to assemble a tailgate party (like the one shown on pages 4 and 5). Start by deciding what nonfood essentials you'll need and pack those first.

Because you won't be using picnic tables in the stadium parking lot, you'll want to pack lawn chairs, a blanket, or plastic ground cloth to sit on. You'll also need a tablecloth, napkins, plastic or paper plates and cups, plastic or regular flatware, moist towelettes, serving utensils, and plastic or paper garbage bags.

Pack for convenience and safety. For example, wrap each flatware setting in a napkin to keep it from rattling in your picnic basket and to speed up "table" setting. Or, use the ground cloth or tablecloth as a wrapper to protect any glass containers.

Avoid taking creamed foods such as custards, puddings, and cream pies because they are susceptible to bacterial growth. Pack the foods for the tailgate party last thing before leaving home. Have everything tightly wrapped. Make sure cold foods are well chilled in advance and kept cold in a cooler. Also, be sure to keep warm foods warm.

Tailgate Coleslaw

Pictured on pages 4–5.

3 cups shredded cabbage **1 cup shredded carrot** **½ cup sliced cucumber** **2 tablespoons sliced green onion**	● In a large bowl toss together the shredded cabbage, shredded carrot, sliced cucumber, and sliced green onion.
¼ cup vinegar **2 tablespoons brown sugar** **1 tablespoon salad oil** **½ teaspoon dry mustard** **½ teaspoon salt**	● In a screw-top jar combine vinegar, brown sugar, salad oil, dry mustard, and salt. Cover and shake well. Pour over combined vegetables. Toss to coat vegetables. Cover and refrigerate for 3 to 24 hours. Toss before serving. Makes 8 side-dish servings.

Use the side of the shredder with large holes to shred the cabbage for Tailgate Coleslaw.

Italian-Style Pasta Salad

1½ quarts water ¼ teaspoon salt 4 ounces spaghetti	● In a large saucepan bring water and salt to a rolling boil. Break the spaghetti in half. Add the spaghetti to the boiling water a little at a time so water does not stop boiling. Reduce heat slightly and continue boiling, uncovered, for 10 to 12 minutes or till the spaghetti is tender, but still slightly firm. Stir occasionally. Drain the spaghetti in a colander. Set aside.
1 6-ounce jar marinated artichoke hearts ½ of a small zucchini	● In a colander drain artichokes; reserve marinade. Coarsely chop artichokes. Halve zucchini lengthwise. Slice halves.
1 cup shredded mozzarella cheese (4 ounces) 1 medium carrot, shredded 2 ounces sliced salami, cut into strips 2 tablespoons grated Parmesan cheese	● In a large bowl combine the cooked spaghetti, chopped artichoke hearts, sliced zucchini, shredded mozzarella cheese, shredded carrot, salami strips, and grated Parmesan cheese.
2 tablespoons salad oil 2 tablespoons white wine vinegar ¾ teaspoon dry mustard ½ teaspoon dried oregano, crushed ½ teaspoon dried basil, crushed 1 clove garlic, minced	● In a screw-top jar combine the reserved artichoke marinade, salad oil, white wine vinegar, dry mustard, dried oregano, dried basil, and minced garlic. Cover tightly and shake well. Pour over spaghetti mixture; toss to coat evenly. Cover and chill for several hours or overnight. Toss before serving. Makes 8 side-dish servings.

Substitute Italian-Style Pasta Salad for the Tailgate Coleslaw at your next Tailgate Party.

Legend has it that Marco Polo took pasta home to Italy from the Orient in the thirteenth century. However, some Italians argue vehemently that pasta was eaten in Rome well before Polo ever set out on his journey. The first pasta seen in the United States was introduced by Thomas Jefferson in 1786, when he brought from Italy an early version of a pasta machine. It wasn't until much later, however, that pasta gained its popularity.

Mexican Brunch

Lazy weekends are perfect for this hearty brunch since some of the food is made ahead. Stuff a tortilla with eggs and chorizo. Serve up fruit and refried beans. It all adds up to a great meal.

Refried Beans
(see recipe, page 13)

Breakfast Burritos
(see recipe, page 13)

Fruit Compote
(see recipe, page 12)

Mock Tequila Sunrise
(see recipe, page 12)

Mexican Brunch

MENU

Breakfast Burritos

Refried Beans

Fruit Compote

Mock Tequila Sunrise

MENU COUNTDOWN

5 Days Ahead:
If desired, prepare Flour Tortillas and Homemade Chorizo for the Breakfast Burritos. Freeze tortillas and Chorizo according to directions in each recipe.
2 Days Ahead:
Prepare Ranchero Salsa for burritos. Cover and chill.

1 Day Ahead:
Prepare Fruit Compote and chill. Prepare Refried Beans.
40 Minutes Ahead:
Prepare burritos. Reheat beans.
Just Before Brunch:
Spoon compote into bowls. Prepare Mock Tequila Sunrise.

Fruit Compote

Pictured on pages 10–11.

½ teaspoon finely shredded orange peel
2 medium oranges
3 cups peeled and sectioned grapefruit; peeled and cut-up papaya; peeled and sliced kiwi fruit; halved strawberries; seedless grapes; *or* fresh pitted dark sweet cherries
2 tablespoons honey
¼ teaspoon ground cinnamon

● Set orange peel aside. Peel and slice oranges crosswise. Place orange slices and remaining desired fruit into a plastic bag, then set the bag in a bowl.

In a small bowl combine honey, cinnamon, and orange peel. Pour honey mixture over fruit in bag. Close bag tightly, then turn to evenly distribute honey mixture. Chill overnight, turning bag occasionally.

To serve, spoon fruit mixture into individual bowls. Makes 6 servings.

Prep time for this compote will vary, depending on whether you peel and section grapefruit, halve strawberries, or use whole grapes.

Mock Tequila Sunrise

Pictured on pages 10–11.

2 cups unsweetened orange juice
1 cup apricot nectar
3 tablespoons lemon juice
Ice cubes
3 tablespoons grenadine syrup
Lime wedges

● In a small pitcher combine orange juice, apricot nectar, and lemon juice. Pour over ice in glasses. Slowly add *1½ teaspoons* grenadine syrup to *each* glass and let it sink to the bottom. Garnish with lime wedges. Stir before drinking. Makes about 6 (4-ounce) servings.

If your taste is more spririted, toast your brunch guests with purchased sangria instead of this nonalcoholic orange juice drink.

Breakfast Burritos

Pictured on pages 10–11.

¼	**pound bulk chorizo**
2	**medium potatoes, peeled and finely chopped (about 2 cups)**
½	**cup chopped onion**
½	**cup chopped sweet red *or* green pepper**
1	**4-ounce can diced green chili peppers, drained**
6	**10-inch flour tortillas**

● For filling, in a 10-inch skillet cook chorizo till it begins to brown. Stir in potatoes, onion, sweet pepper, and chili peppers. Cook, covered, over medium-low heat for 12 to 15 minutes or till potatoes are tender, stirring occasionally. Drain off fat.

Stack tortillas and wrap tightly in foil. Heat in a 350° oven for 10 minutes to soften. (When ready to fill tortillas, remove only *half* at a time, keeping remaining ones warm in oven.)

6	**beaten eggs**
½	**cup shredded Monterey Jack cheese (2 ounces)**
¼	**teaspoon salt**
⅛	**teaspoon pepper**
2	**tablespoons butter *or* margarine**

● Meanwhile, in a medium mixing bowl combine eggs, cheese, salt, and pepper.

In an 8-inch skillet melt butter or margarine over medium heat, then pour in egg mixture. Cook, without stirring, till mixture begins to set on the bottom and around edges. Lift and fold partially cooked eggs so uncooked portion flows underneath. Continue cooking over medium heat for 4 to 5 minutes or till eggs are cooked throughout but are still glossy and moist. Remove from heat.

1	**medium tomato, chopped**

● Spoon about *½ cup* potato mixture onto *each* tortilla just below center. Top *each* with some of the egg mixture, then sprinkle with a little tomato. Fold bottom edge of each tortilla up and over filling just till mixture is covered. Fold opposite sides of each tortilla in, just till they meet. Roll up tortillas from the bottom. Secure with wooden toothpicks.

Shredded lettuce
Salsa *or* taco sauce
Refried Beans (optional) (see recipe, right)

● Arrange burritos on a baking sheet. Bake in a 350° oven for 10 to 12 minutes or till heated through.

Remove toothpicks. Serve burritos on lettuce with Ranchero Salsa and Refried Beans, if desired. Makes 6 servings.

Refried Beans: In a Dutch oven combine 1 pound *dry pinto beans* and 6 cups *water.* Bring to boiling. Reduce heat and simmer for 2 minutes. Remove from heat. Cover and let stand for 1 hour. (Or, soak beans in water overnight in a covered pan.) Drain.

In same Dutch oven combine drained beans and 4 cups additional *water.* Bring to boiling. Cover and simmer for 2 hours or till very tender.

In a large heavy skillet heat ¼ cup *bacon drippings or cooking oil.* Add beans with liquid, 1½ teaspoons *salt,* and 2 cloves *garlic,* minced.

Using a potato masher, mash bean mixture completely. Cook, uncovered, for 10 to 15 minutes or till thick, stirring often. Makes 8 to 10 side-dish servings or about 5 cups.

Mocha Almond Mousse
(see recipe, page 19)

Fire Up a Fiesta

When it comes to hosting a successful dinner party, let the old Mexican saying "Mi casa es su casa"—My house is your house—set the mood. Welcome your guests with mariachi (Mexican street band) music, brightly colored decorations, and this easy-on-the-cook-but-oh-so-delicious menu.

Marinated Zucchini Salad
(see recipe, page 16)

Avocado Soup
(see recipe, page 17)

Bolillos
(see recipe, page 18)

**Fillets Stuffed with
Peppers and Cheese**
(see recipe, page 17)

Fire Up a Fiesta

MENU

Avocado Soup

Fillets Stuffed with Peppers
  and Cheese

Marinated Zucchini Salad

Bolillos
(see recipe, page 18)

Mocha Almond Mousse
(see recipe, page 19)

MENU COUNTDOWN

1 Week Ahead:
Prepare Bolillos. Wrap in
heavy-duty foil and freeze.
1 Day Ahead:
Prepare Marinated Zucchini
Salad. Cover and chill.
Prepare Mocha Almond
Mousse. Spoon into dessert
dishes and chill.
Morning of Party:
Remove rolls from freezer
to thaw (leave rolls in foil).
About 3 Hours Ahead:
Prepare Avocado Soup.
Cover and chill.
About 45 Minutes Ahead:
Light charcoal. Assemble
Fillets Stuffed with Peppers
and Cheese. Cover; chill.

15 Minutes Ahead:
Transfer soup to a
saucepan. Cook and stir till
heated through. Thin soup
to desired consistency by
adding a little light cream or
milk, if necessary.
12 to 14 Minutes Ahead:
Start grilling the fillets.
Leaving rolls wrapped in
foil, reheat in a 325° oven
or, if there's room, reheat
alongside fillets on grill.
10 Minutes Ahead:
Transfer salad to a serving
platter.
Before Serving Dessert:
Add whipped cream and
almonds to desserts.

Marinated Zucchini Salad

Pictured on pages 14–15.

½ cup white wine vinegar
½ cup olive oil *or* salad oil
2 teaspoons sugar
1 teaspoon dried basil,
    crushed
¼ teaspoon salt
1 clove garlic, minced
2 small zucchini, halved
    lengthwise and sliced
    ¼ inch thick (2 cups)
1 cup canned garbanzo
    beans, drained
¼ cup sliced pitted ripe
    olives

● For marinade, in a screw-top jar
combine vinegar, oil, sugar, basil, salt,
and garlic. Cover and shake well.
  In a medium mixing bowl stir together
zucchini, garbanzo beans, and olives.
Pour marinade over zucchini mixture,
stirring to coat. Cover and refrigerate
for at least 3 hours or overnight,
stirring occasionally.

**For a more piquant flavor,
try pimiento-stuffed olives
instead of ripe olives.**

Lettuce leaves
2 tablespoons sliced green
    onion
2 medium tomatoes, cut
    into wedges

● To serve, drain zucchini mixture,
reserving marinade. Spoon zucchini
mixture onto a lettuce-lined platter and
top with green onion and tomato
wedges. Drizzle with a little of the
reserved marinade. Makes 6 servings.

Fillets Stuffed With Peppers And Cheese

Pictured on pages 14–15.

3 or 4 large Anaheim
    peppers, chopped, *or*
    two 4-ounce cans diced
    green chili peppers,
    drained
1 cup chopped onion
2 cloves garlic, minced
1 tablespoon cooking oil
½ cup shredded Monterey
    Jack cheese (2 ounces)
3 tablespoons fine dry bread
    crumbs
6 beef tenderloin steaks,
    cut 1 inch thick
    (about 2½ pounds)
  Salt
  Pepper

● For stuffing, in a large skillet cook peppers, onion, and garlic in oil till tender but not brown. Remove from heat and stir in cheese and bread crumbs.

Meanwhile, cut a pocket in each steak about 3 inches long and 1½ to 2 inches deep (see top photo, right). Season pockets with salt and pepper.

Put about *2 tablespoons* stuffing mixture into *each* steak pocket. Fasten pocket openings with wooden toothpicks (see bottom photo, right). Cover and chill, if desired.

Use a sharp knife to cut a pocket in each fillet that's about 3 inches long and 1½ to 2 inches deep.

● Grill steaks, on an uncovered grill, directly over *medium* coals for 5 minutes. Turn and grill to desired doneness, allowing 7 to 9 minutes more for medium. Or, broil 3 to 4 inches from heat to desired doneness, turning once (allow about 12 minutes total time for medium). Makes 6 servings.

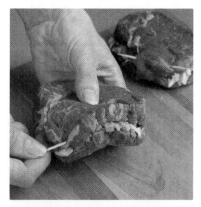

Securely close pocket openings with wooden toothpicks.

Avocado Soup

Pictured on pages 14–15.

1 14½-ounce can chicken
    broth
1 cup light cream
1 large avocado, seeded,
    peeled, and cut up
1 small onion, cut up
2 tablespoons dry sherry
  Few dashes bottled hot
    pepper sauce
  Dairy sour cream
  Snipped cilantro *or*
    parsley (optional)

● In a blender container combine the chicken broth, light cream, avocado, onion, sherry, and bottled hot pepper sauce. Cover and blend till smooth. Cover and chill, if desired.

Transfer the avocado mixture to a medium saucepan. Cook and stir over medium heat about 10 minutes or till heated through.

Dollop with sour cream and garnish with cilantro or parsley, if desired. Makes 6 side-dish servings.

Remember this soup during the next heat wave. Serve it cold with a salad or sandwich—it makes a light, refreshing supper.

Bolillos

Pictured on pages 14–15.

7 to 7¼ cups all-purpose flour **2 packages active dry yeast** **2½ cups water** **1 tablespoon sugar** **1 tablespoon shortening** **½ teaspoon salt**	● In a large mixer bowl combine *3 cups* of the flour and yeast. In a medium saucepan heat the water, sugar, shortening, and salt just till warm (115° to 120°) and shortening is almost melted, stirring constantly. Add to flour mixture. Beat with an electric mixer on low speed for ½ minute, scraping sides of bowl constantly. Beat 3 minutes at high speed. Stir in as much of the remaining flour as you can mix in with a spoon.
	● Turn dough out onto a lightly floured surface. Knead in enough of the remaining flour to make a stiff dough that is smooth and elastic (8 to 10 minutes total). Shape into a ball. Place in a lightly greased bowl. Turn dough once to grease surface. Cover and let rise in a warm place till double (1 to 1½ hours).
Yellow cornmeal	● Punch dough down. Cover and let rest for 10 minutes. Divide into 18 portions. Shape each into an oval about 5 inches long. Pull and twist ends slightly (see top photo, right). Sprinkle cornmeal over 2 greased baking sheets. Transfer rolls to baking sheets. Use a sharp knife to make a cut, ¼ inch deep, down center of each roll (see bottom photo, right).
1 egg white **1 tablespoon water**	● Combine egg white and water. Brush tops and sides of rolls with egg-white-water mixture. Cover and let rise till nearly double (about 45 minutes). Bake in a 375° oven for 20 minutes. Brush again with egg-white-water mixture. Bake for 10 to 12 minutes more or till golden brown Cool on wire racks. Makes 18 rolls.

On a lightly floured surface, roll each portion of dough with the palms of your hands into an oval. Pull and twist each end.

Slash each roll lengthwise with a sharp knife, making cuts about ¼ inch deep.

Mocha Almond Mousse

Pictured on pages 14–15.

¼ **cup sugar** 2 **teaspoons instant coffee crystals** 1 **envelope unflavored gelatin** 1¾ **cups milk** 4 **squares (4 ounces) semisweet chocolate, cut up**	● In a medium saucepan combine sugar, coffee crystals, and gelatin. Stir in milk and chocolate. Cook and stir over low heat till crystals dissolve and chocolate melts.
4 **beaten egg yolks** ¼ **cup coffee liqueur** ¼ **teaspoon almond extract**	● Gradually stir about *half* of the hot milk mixture into egg yolks, then return all to saucepan. Cook and stir for 2 to 3 minutes or till slightly thickened. *Do not boil.* Remove from heat and stir in coffee liqueur and almond extract. Chill gelatin mixture to the consistency of corn syrup, stirring occasionally. Remove from the refrigerator (gelatin mixture will continue to set up).
4 **egg whites** 2 **tablespoons sugar** ½ **cup whipping cream** **Whipped cream** **Sliced almonds**	● Immediately beat egg whites till soft peaks form (tips curl). Gradually add sugar, beating till stiff peaks form (tips stand straight). When gelatin mixture is partially set (consistency of unbeaten egg whites), fold in stiffly beaten egg whites. Beat ½ cup whipping cream till soft peaks form, then fold into gelatin mixture. Chill till mixture mounds slightly when spooned. Transfer to dessert dishes and chill for several hours or overnight. To serve, dollop with whipped cream and garnish with almonds. Serves 6 to 8.

No room in the fridge for all those dessert dishes? Save space by chilling the mousse in a 1½-quart soufflé dish.

House-to-House Halloween

A knock at your door—the witches, goblins, and ghosts have arrived. It's Halloween! And there's no better way to celebrate than with a progressive party. Get together with your neighbors or friends to plan the fun. Begin the journey with a warm meal of Witch's Spell, Corny-Meal Muffins, Pumpkin Patch Cookies, and Spook 'n' Cider. Then proceed to the second, third, and fourth house for an evening full of games and treats. (See recipes and tips, pages 22 to 25.)

MENU
Witch's Spell
Corny-Meal Muffins
Pumpkin Patch Cookies
Spook 'n' Cider

TREATS
Roasted Pumpkin Seeds
Popcorn Logs
Goblins' Gorp

Witch's Spell

Pictured on pages 20–21.

6 14½-ounce cans
     chicken broth
4 medium carrots, thinly
     sliced
2 medium cooking apples,
     peeled, cored, and
     chopped (about
     2 cups)
½ cup chopped celery
½ cup chopped green pepper
1 teaspoon dried thyme,
     crushed

● In a medium Dutch oven combine broth, carrots, apples, celery, green pepper, and thyme. Bring mixture to boiling, then reduce heat. Cover and simmer for 10 minutes.

3 cups diced cooked
     chicken
1 cup alphabet pasta

● Stir in chicken and pasta. Bring to boiling again, then reduce heat. Cover and simmer about 10 minutes more or till vegetables and pasta are tender. Makes 16 servings.

Corny-Meal Muffins

2 beaten eggs
1 8¾-ounce can cream-style
     corn
⅓ cup milk
¾ cup shredded cheddar
     cheese (3 ounces)
2 7- *or* 8½-ounce packages
     corn muffin mix

● Grease muffin pans or line with paper bake cups. Set pans aside.
   In a medium mixing bowl combine eggs, corn, and milk. Stir in cheese. Add dry muffin mix and stir till moistened (batter should be lumpy).

● Fill each cup two-thirds full. Bake in a 400° oven for 15 to 20 minutes or till a wooden toothpick comes out clean and the tops are slightly golden. Cool muffins in the pans for 5 minutes. If necessary, loosen carefully with a knife. Remove muffins from pans. Serve warm or cool completely. Makes 16 servings.

MENU COUNTDOWN
2 days ahead:
House 2—Begin to prepare Roasted Pumpkin Seeds.
1 day ahead:
House 1—Bake Pumpkin Patch Cookies. Store in a covered container.
House 2—Finish preparing and packaging Roasted Pumpkin Seeds.
House 3—Prepare and wrap Popcorn Logs.
House 4—Prepare and package Goblins' Gorp.
Several hours ahead:
House 1—Decorate cookies.
   Prepare Spook 'n' Cider. Cover and chill.
About 1 hour ahead:
House 1—Begin to prepare Witch's Spell.
   Prepare Corny-Meal Muffins.
Just before serving:
House 1—Heat Spook 'n' Cider.
After supper:
House 2—Have a pumpkin race giving Roasted Pumpkin Seeds as treats.
House 3—Create a mystery, giving Popcorn Logs as treats.
House 4—Have a goblin hunt giving Goblins' Gorp as treats.

Pumpkin Patch Cookies

Pictured on pages 20–21.

3½	cups all-purpose flour
1	teaspoon baking powder

● In a medium mixing bowl stir together flour and baking powder. Set flour mixture aside.

1½	cups butter *or* margarine
¼	teaspoon orange paste food coloring
1	cup sugar

● In a large mixer bowl beat butter or margarine and food coloring with an electric mixer on medium speed till butter is softened and food coloring is blended in (about 30 seconds). Add sugar and beat till fluffy.

1	egg
1	teaspoon vanilla

● Add egg and vanilla, then beat well. Stir in flour mixture. *Do not chill dough.*

● Put the flower plate onto a cookie press. Pack dough, half at a time, into the cookie press. Press dough into flowers on ungreased cookie sheets.

● Bake in a 400° oven for 7 to 8 minutes or till cookies are just light brown around edges. Remove cookies to a wire rack, then cool completely.

1	cup creamy chocolate frosting *(use a creamy fudge frosting mix for a 1-layer cake)*
18	green jelly beans, cut crosswise in half

● Spread the flat side of *half* of the cookies with some frosting. Top with remaining cookies to form pumpkins.

For stems, attach one jelly bean half to the top of each cookie with frosting.

Let stand for 1 to 2 hours or till frosting is slightly dry. Makes 36.

As the kids arrive, keep them busy by having them make their own treat bags. They can color small paper bags, then staple on orange or black strips of construction paper for easy-carrying handles. And for their first treat, slip a few *Pumpkin Patch Cookies* into each bag.

Spook 'n' Cider

10 cups apple cider *or* apple juice 1 12-ounce package frozen red raspberries (lightly sweetened) 5 inches stick cinnamon	● In a large saucepan combine apple cider or juice, raspberries, and cinnamon. Bring to boiling, then reduce heat. Cover and simmer for 10 minutes. Remove mixture from heat. Strain berries and cinnamon from mixture through a piece of cheesecloth. Cover till serving time.	Boo! You can create a spooky sight by filling jack-o'-lanterns with dry ice and a little water— vapor will float out of the jack-o'-lantern. When using the dry ice, be sure that you're in a well ventilated area and protect your hands by wearing heavy gloves.
	● To serve, heat cider mixture till warm. Makes 16 (5-ounce) servings.	

Roasted Pumpkin Seeds

4¼ cups raw pumpkin seeds 2 tablespoons cooking oil 1 teaspoon salt	● Rinse pumpkin seeds in water till pulp and strings are washed off, then drain. In a medium mixing bowl combine pumpkin seeds, cooking oil, and salt. Spread mixture onto a waxed-paper-lined 15x10x1-inch baking pan. Let stand for 24 to 48 hours or till dry, stirring occasionally.	Plan on using the seeds from about four pumpkins for this recipe. If you don't have enough, ask your friends to share the seeds from their pumpkins with you.
	● Remove waxed paper from baking pan. Toast seeds in a 325° oven for 40 minutes, stirring once or twice. Drain seeds on paper towels.	Use this crunchy snack for prizes in a pumpkin race. Divide the kids into two groups. Give each group a pumpkin and have the kids race by rolling the pumpkin with their feet, hands, or noses.
16 small clear plastic bags *or* 6-inch-square pieces of colored cellophane wrap Ribbon	● Package ¼ cup of the seeds in each bag or place seeds in the center of cellophane wrap, then bring up edges. Tie closed with the ribbon. Makes 16 (¼-cup) servings.	

Popcorn Logs

14 cups popped popcorn	● Remove all unpopped kernels from popped corn. Place popcorn in a greased 17x12x2-inch baking pan. Keep popcorn warm in a 300° oven while making syrup mixture.
1 cup sugar ½ cup water ½ cup light molasses ¼ teaspoon salt	● Butter the sides of a heavy 2-quart saucepan. In the saucepan combine sugar, water, molasses, and salt. Cook over medium-high heat till boiling, stirring constantly. Reduce heat to medium. Clip a candy thermometer to the side of the pan. 　Continue cooking over medium heat, stirring occasionally, till thermometer registers 250° (hard-ball stage), watching carefully to prevent the syrup from boiling over.
1 cup sunflower nuts	● Pour syrup mixture over popcorn. Add sunflower nuts and stir gently to coat popcorn. Cool mixture until easy to handle. Use buttered hands to shape mixture into sixteen 3½-inch logs. Cool logs completely.
Clear plastic wrap *or* colored cellophane wrap Ribbon	● Wrap each log in clear plastic or colored cellophane wrap. Tie ends closed with ribbon. Makes 16 servings.

Get your guests involved in creating a mystery. First gather everyone in a circle. Dim the lights, but keep the jack-o'-lanterns lit. Then start by making up a mystery tale. But before you finish it, turn to the child next to you and have him add onto the story. Continue adding onto the mystery until everyone has taken a turn.

Goblins' Gorp

3½ cups honey graham cereal 1½ cups peanuts 1½ cups raisins 1½ cups candy-coated milk chocolate pieces	● In a large mixing bowl combine honey graham cereal, peanuts, raisins, and chocolate pieces.
16 small clear plastic bags *or* 12-inch-square pieces of colored cellophane wrap Ribbon	● Package ½ cup of the mixture in each bag or place mixture in the center of the cellophane wrap, then bring up edges. Tie closed with ribbon. Makes 16 (½-cup) servings.

When the little ones come to your house, have a goblin hunt. Draw small pictures of goblins on paper and attach them to a treat. Then hide the packages. When all of the treats are found, send the kids to the next house.

Wine and Cheese Party—Cheese Sampler

Next time you're planning a get-together, make it a wine-and-cheese-tasting party! It's a fun and easy way to get acquainted with a variety of wines and cheeses. Use the information on this and the next five pages to help you decide what wines and cheeses to serve together. Then, if you like, round out the party with one or two of the appetizers on pages 32 and 33.

To serve the cheese, plan about ¼ pound cheese per person. Remove the cheeses from the refrigerator about an hour before serving so they will be at their flavor-peak. Set out unsalted crackers and fresh fruit to nibble between tastings. Choose as many cheeses as you like from these two pages (also see photo, pages 28 and 29), being sure to include a balance of strong and mild cheeses as well as textures ranging from soft to hard.

Asiago (ah-see-AH-goh) is a hard cheese with a strong, sharp, and slightly salty flavor. It may or may not be coated with paraffin. Thinly sliced, the cheese is good for sandwiches or snacks, but also can be grated and used like grated Parmesan cheese.

Bel Paese (bel-pah-AY-say) is the consistency of firm butter. It has a slightly gray surface and a creamy yellow interior. The flavor ranges from delicately rich, sweet, and creamy to robust. Serve it with fruit and crackers, or use it like mozzarella in sauces or casseroles.

Blue cheese is the name used for several varieties of blue-veined cheeses. Even though they are all called blue-veined, some cheeses actually can have blue, blue-black, or green veins. Blue cheese is strong and pungent in flavor. Use it in salads and salad dressings or with fruit.

Boursin (boor-SOHN) is a rich, creamy, tangy cheese that is flavored with pepper, garlic, or herbs. In its natural state, boursin is pure white, but when flavorings are added, its color depends upon the flavoring. Serve boursin as an appetizer.

Brick cheese has a mild, sweetish tasting flavor, but at the same time, it has a certain pungency, tanginess, and distinctive aroma. Brick cheese can be aged for up to three months. The younger the cheese, the milder the flavor and the creamier the texture. Serve brick cheese as an appetizer or in sandwiches.

Brie (bree) cheese has a creamy, rich flavor that is both subtle and tangy at the same time. The thin, edible crust is a powdery white, while the interior color varies from cream to golden. Serve Brie with fruit or as an appetizer.

Bruder Basil (BREW-der BAZ-el) is a German cheese with a slightly smoky flavor. It's traditionally served around the holidays as an appetizer.

Camembert (KAM-ehm-berh) is slightly bitter and yeasty in flavor. When the cheese is cut, the soft, almost-fluid consistency of the cheese causes it to bulge out from under its white to off-white edible crust. Serve Camembert as an appetizer or as a dessert with fruit.

Cheddar cheese is naturally white, but usually is colored deep golden-yellow. It frequently is labeled as being mild, medium, or sharp in flavor, with the longer-aged cheddars sharper and more full-bodied. Cheddar is an all-purpose cheese that can be used in salads, sandwiches, sauces, main dishes, or with fruits.

Cheshire (CHEHSH-er) cheese is a crumbly, white- to orange-colored cheese with a musty aroma. The flavor is tangy yet mild. Serve it as an appetizer, a snack, or in sandwiches.

Colby cheese has a texture similar to cheddar cheese, but slightly more granular. The flavor is slightly sweeter than cheddar, but grows stronger with age. This golden-yellow cheese can be used as a snack, or in sandwiches, sauces, or casseroles.

Edam (EE-dam) is a firm-textured cheese shaped into a flattened ball and coated with red paraffin. It has a mild and nutty flavor that works well in appetizers, desserts, or main dishes.

Farmer cheese varies widely in both texture and flavor. Depending on the age of the cheese, it may be dry and crumbly with a slight bitterness or tang, while others are creamy with a very mild flavor. Serve it in salads or with fruit.

Feta (FEHT-ah) is a traditional, soft, white, Greek cheese with a sharp, salty flavor. Its crumbly texture appears wet but feels dry. If you find its flavor to be too sharp or salty, soak it in milk. Serve feta in salads, sandwiches, or casseroles.

Fontina (fon-TEE-nah) has a delicate nutty flavor and a pleasant aroma. This wheel-shaped cheese may have small holes scattered over its smooth, shiny surface. Serve fontina as an appetizer, snack, dessert, or in fondues or casseroles.

Gjetost (YET-ohst), a Norwegian goat cheese, has a distinctive rich brown color and a hard, solid texture. Its color and sweet caramelized flavor are unlike any other cheese. Serve thinly sliced gjetost with fruit or on breads.

Gorgonzola (gor-gon-ZOH-lah), an off-white cheese with greenish-blue veins, has a strong, pungent flavor and aroma. It is creamy and salty, but less salty than blue cheese. Use it as you would other blue cheeses.

Gouda (GOO-dah) has a yellow-orange interior and is coated with a yellow or red wax. It is shaped like a flattened ball. The flavor is mild and slightly nutty, and its texture is smooth and waxy. Serve it as an appetizer, snack, or dessert, or in salads and sandwiches.

Gruyère (groo-YEHR) has a mild, nutlike flavor with a slightly sweetish aftertaste. It is firm-bodied and has small holes or "eyes." Serve Gruyère with fruit or in appetizers, soups, and fondues.

Havarti (ha-VART-ee) is a cream-colored cheese that varies in flavor. Young havarti (aged two to three months) has a mild flavor. When aged longer, havarti acquires a pungent flavor. It has a porous yellow-to-white texture with small, irregular holes. Serve it as an appetizer or snack, in sandwiches, or as a dessert with fruit.

Jarlsberg (YARLS-berg), with its smooth, firm, texture and small holes, looks similar to Swiss, but has a very mild flavor. The cheese has a thick natural rind covered with a yellow wax. The interior is white to light yellow in color. Serve Jarlsberg with fruit or in sandwiches, sauces, or casseroles.

Limburger cheese is famous for its very pungent aroma and flavor; enjoying it is an acquired taste. It has a pale yellow color and a soft, creamy texture. Serve it as a snack or with strong-flavored vegetables, such as onions, radishes, or shallots.

Montery Jack (MONT-er-ay JAK) cheese has a rather chewy consistency. This creamy-white colored cheese has a mild and nutty flavor. Well known for its use in Mexican cooking, you can also serve it as a snack.

Mozzarella cheese has a mild flavor that is creamy and vaguely sweet. The texture is smooth and firm. Because of its mild flavor and creamy consistency, you can use it in almost all types of cooking.

Muenster (MUHN-ster) cheese varies in texture from moist, porous, and spongy to crumbly and dry. Its flavor varies from mild to pungent. Muenster cheese made in the United States or Denmark is usually the mild and moist variety, and that made in Germany is the drier, crumbly, pungent type. Muenster usually is made in wheels and has a thin outer rind. It can be served as a dessert or snack or in sandwiches.

Parmesan is a straw-yellow cheese that tastes slightly nutty and salty. It is a very dry cheese that is made in large wheels. However, the grated form is the most familiar. Parmesan cheese will stay fresh many months because of its low moisture content. Serve it to complement salads, breads, or main dishes.

Port du Salut (pohr-doo-sah-LOO) cheese at first tastes mild, buttery, creamy, and smooth, but later develops a subtle, sharp aftertaste. It is made in small wheels and has a creamy-yellow interior that is covered by a thin orange rind. Serve it as a snack or dessert.

Provolone (proh-voh-LOH-nee) cheese varies from mild to sharp, and has a lightly smoked flavor. It has a light, golden, interior and a brown surface. The texture is firm, compact, and flaky. Use it in appetizers, sandwiches, or snacks.

Romano cheese is a dry, hard cheese that is similar to Parmesan cheese, but has a stronger flavor and aroma. Romano can be used in salads or sandwiches, as a snack, or in pasta dishes. It is usually grated or shredded like Parmesan cheese.

Roquefort (ROHK-fort) cheese is creamy-white in color, with many blue veins. It has a strong, pungent, salty flavor with a lingering aftertaste. Use it as you would other blue cheeses.

Sage Derby is a variation of Derby cheese. Fresh sage leaves have been added to it, giving it a greenish hue. The sage also adds a sharp, fragrant flavor to the cheese. Use Sage Derby in salad dressings, as an appetizer, or crumble it and sprinkle in soups or salads.

Sapsago (sap-SAY-goh) is an unusual cone-shaped cheese with a hard dry texture and a "grassy" flavor. The light green color comes from the large quantity of dried clover added to the curd. Sapsago is a hard grating cheese that can be used in salads or egg dishes.

Stilton often is referred to as the "king" of the blue-veined cheeses. It has a dense but crumbly texture. The flavor is piquant but rich. It is less salty and milder than Roquefort and is less creamy than Gorgonzola. It has a brown-gray rind that is crusty and slightly wrinkled. Serve Stilton with fruit for dessert or use it in salads.

Swiss is a popular cheese with a firm, smooth texture. There are large holes or "eyes" scattered throughout the cheese. It varies in color from off-white to a rich yellow. The sweet and nutty taste makes Swiss excellent as an appetizer or snack or as an ingredient in casseroles, sandwiches, or salads.

1. Cheddar 2. Stilton 3. Sage Derby 4. Port du Salut
5. Vermont White Cheddar 6. Edam 7. Bel Paese
8. Jarlsberg 9. String Mozzarella 10. Blue Cheese
11. Cheshire with Stilton 12. Provolone 13. Gjetost
14. Bruder Basil 15. Sapsago

Wine and Cheese Party— Wine Sampler

Tailor your wine and cheese party to the types of wines that interest you. For a "first-course" tasting, feature appetizer wines such as sherry and vermouth. A "dessert" tasting can focus on sweet dessert wines such as port or cream sherry. Or, if you like, offer a more varied selection of wines that includes reds, whites, and rosés. Plan on serving 1 ounce of each appetizer or dessert wine per person, and 1 to 2 ounces per person of the others. Suggestions for cheeses to accompany the various wines can be found below.

Burgundy
(BUR-gun-dy)
Technically, Burgundy comes from a legally delimited area in France and includes both red and white wines. Because French law reserves the name "Burgundy" only for certain wines, all French Burgundys are better-than-average wines.

Worldwide, the name burgundy is used to describe any full-bodied red wine. If you're looking for an honorable U.S. counterpart of a true French Burgundy, look for bottles labeled Pinot Noir and Gamay-Beaujolais (red), or Chardonnay (white).

Serve with cheddar, Port du Salut, provolone, or Gorgonzola cheeses.

Beaujolais
(BO-zho-lay)
Beaujolais, made from the Gamay grape, is one of the best-loved red wines from the Lyons region of France. It has a fruity, full-bodied, almost spicy flavor, with no trace of harshness.

Each November, another Beaujolais, *Beaujolais Primeur* (also known as *Nouveau),* is made available. The French call it the "wine of the new year." It is a light, almost fizzing, pale red wine that should be used before New Year's Day. Serve both types of Beaujolais with cheddar cheese.

Cabernet Sauvignon
(kab-er-NAY SO-veen-yon)
This great red wine grape, originally from the Bordeaux region of France, is responsible for the high quality of some of the world's most celebrated wines. In France it becomes some of the classic Clarets of Bordeaux. In American wines, the name Cabernet or Cabernet Sauvignon on a wine label is an indication of a superior red wine.

Try serving Cabernet Sauvignon with Brie, Camembert, sharp cheddar, or blue cheeses.

Champagne
Strictly speaking, Champagne means French Champagne: a wine made from only certain varieties of grapes, in a legally delimited region of France.

Other countries have adopted other names for their own sparkling wines, as *sekt* in Germany and *spumante* in Italy. However, in the U.S., any sparkling wine may be called champagne provided it's made by the same bottle-fermented process as French Champagne, and its geographic origin is on the label.

According to the degree of dryness of the wine, champagne may be labeled as follows:
Brut: the driest and least sweet
Extra-Dry: not as dry as brut
Sec: slightly sweet
Demi-Sec: quite sweet

Serve champagnes with Brie or cream cheeses.

Chablis
(shab-LEE)
In France, Chablis is a white wine from the Burgundy region. It has an intensely dry, almost harsh flavor. Its color is a light yellow, with a slightly greenish overtone.

In the U.S., any white table wine can be called "chablis." To find a California counterpart for the fine French wine, look for bottles labeled Chardonnay or Pinot Chardonnay. Serve any chablis with Edam, Gouda, or brick cheeses.

Chenin Blanc
(SHEN-in BLAWN)
This grape is used to make such French white wines as Vouvray and Anjou Blanc. The wines are soft, slightly dry, and nicely fruity.

In the U.S., this varietal wine is sometimes a little sweet with a pleasing perfumed aroma. Serve with Gouda, Edam, or Swiss cheeses.

Chianti
(key-AHN-tee)
Chianti is a red Italian table wine that's famous worldwide, thanks to its straw-covered bottle (fiasco). Within the Chianti region of Italy is a strictly delimited zone where wines may be labeled *Chianti Classico*. Only a *Chianti Classico* carries a seal which consists of a black target with a rooster in the center and varying colors of borders (the border's color indicates the number of years of aging).

California chianti—with or without the fancy bottle—is a blend of red wines. It is ruby red, medium tart, and medium-bodied. Serve chianti with blue cheeses.

French Colombard
Colombard is a productive, good-quality white wine grape, grown principally in the Cognac district of France. In France, it gives an agreeable, though not very distinguished, dry white wine.

In California, this wine is green-gold in color, and has a light, delicate flavor with just enough acid to stimulate the taste buds. Serve with Gouda, Swiss, or Muenster cheeses.

Gewürztraminer
(geb-vert-tra-MEAN-er or geb-woors-tra-mean-AIR)
This tough-skinned, pinkish-blue grape, well known in Germany and the Alsace region of France, makes a distinctive white wine. Spicy and aromatic—there's no mistaking this wine. It's the one you'll remember as "perfumy," and for some people it takes a while to appreciate. The same qualities, though somewhat muted, are found in the American-grown grape. Serve with boursin, Edam, Monterey Jack, Gouda, or Muenster cheeses.

Pinot Noir
(pea-no NWAR)
The Pinot Noir grape is responsible for all fine red French Burgundys. On a California label, Pinot usually assures an above-average wine. A good Pinot Noir is smooth, soft, and light in character. Serve with Gorgonzola, Stilton, or blue cheeses.

Port
Port is a rich, full-bodied wine made in red, white, and amber colors. To make port, fermentation of the original wine is halted with brandy. Ports aged in wooden casks for two or more years are labeled as *ruby* or *tawny*. Tawny is older, browner, less fruity, and usually more expensive than ruby port. *Vintage* port is aged in bottles for at least 10 years after it's been aged in casks for two years.

Serve ruby or tawny port with Edam, Gouda, cream cheese, cheddar, or Camembert cheeses.

Riesling
(REES-ling)
The Riesling grape, from Germany's Rhine and Mosel valleys, is one of the greatest of white wine grapes. The German wine is slightly sweet to very sweet.

In the U.S., wines from the classic German Riesling grape are labeled Johannisberg Riesling or White Riesling. They have a floral aroma, a clean fruity taste, and a good balance of acidity along with a slight sweetness. Other U.S. wines may be labeled riesling if they contain a *variety* of the Riesling grape, such as Grey Riesling or Emerald Riesling. Serve with Muenster, Gouda, or Gruyère cheeses.

Rosé Wines
(ro-ZAY)
Rosé wines are simply pale red wines. The grape skins are removed early in fermentation, before all the usual red color can develop in the wine. Rosés may be sweet or dry or even lightly carbonated. Rosés are produced in almost all wine-growing countries.

There are as many tastes as there are grapes and blends of rosé. The finest rosés are dry, fruity, and fresh tasting. Rosé wines are most flavorful, with their loveliest color, within two years of vintage—so don't try to age them. Serve with mild cheeses such as brick, mozzarella, Muenster, or Jarlsberg.

Sauvignon Blanc
(SO-vee-nyawn BLAWN)
One of the white wine grapes from the Bordeaux region of France, the Sauvignon Blanc grape is used to make the dry wines of Sancerre and Pouilly-Fumé. In the U.S., both dry and sweet Sauvignon Blancs are produced. Some of the dry ones are labeled Fumé Blanc or Blanc Fumé.

Sauvignon Blanc is aromatic, a little spicy, and very fruity. Serve with farmer cheeses or with Swiss or Gruyère cheeses.

Sherry
Sherry is made in many countries of the world, but true sherry comes from Spain. It is a fortified wine, which means that brandy is added before bottling to bring the alcohol content to about 20 percent.

Sherry comes dry or sweet, with many gradations between:
Fino: light and dry; usually served before dinner
Amontillado: medium dry
Manzanilla: very pale and dry
Oloroso: dark and medium-sweet
Cream: sweetened Oloroso

Dry sherries pair nicely with blue cheeses and also with sharp and extra-sharp cheddars. Serve cream sherries with Camembert, Edam, Gouda, or Muenster cheeses.

Vermouth
(ver-MOOTH)
Vermouth is used today principally as an aperitif and as a cocktail ingredient. It's made by adding brandy to wine, then flavoring it with a mixture of up to 50 herbs. Each vermouth manufacturer has his own special recipe.

There are two kinds of vermouth: dry and sweet. Dry vermouth is highly perfumed with herbs and spices and is added sparingly to martini cocktails. Sweet vermouth also has flavorings added, but is mellower and more robust. It is used in manhattan cocktails. Serve dry vermouth with Brie or mild cheddar cheeses.

Zinfandel
(ZIN-fan-dell)
Although it may have Italian origin, Zinfandel is a long-time California specialty grape that's now gaining recognition and popularity. These red wine grapes produce a distinctive wine that may be enjoyed as either a young or aged table wine—or even as a rich, late-harvest wine.

When young, Zinfandel tastes fruity and dry, with a berrylike aroma and flavor. If aged, the bouquet suggests black currants, pepper, herbs, and spice. Serve with Monterey Jack, Edam, Port du Salut, or Bel Paese cheeses.

Mini Quiches

Pictured on the cover.

1 package (6) refrigerated flaky dinner rolls	● Separate each dinner roll into 4 layers. Place *each* section in a greased 1¾-inch-diameter muffin cup, pressing the dough onto bottom and up sides of muffin cup. Sprinkle *1 teaspoon* cheese into *each* muffin cup. Sprinkle *1 rounded teaspoon* crab over cheese.
½ cup shredded Swiss cheese (2 ounces)	
1 6-ounce can crab meat, drained, flaked, and cartilage removed	
1 egg	● In a bowl combine egg, milk, and dillweed. Spoon about *1½ teaspoons* egg mixture into *each* muffin cup.
½ cup milk	
½ teaspoon dried dillweed	
	● Bake in a 375° oven about 20 minutes or till golden. Remove from pans. Serve warm. Makes 24.

Refrigerated dinner rolls speed up putting together these extra-flaky two-bite morsels.

Beef Turnovers

½ pound ground beef	● For filling, in a 10-inch skillet brown ground beef. Drain well. Stir in spinach, mushrooms, catsup, basil, thyme, and ¼ teaspoon *salt.* Set filling aside.
½ cup chopped cooked spinach, well-drained	
1 3-ounce can chopped mushrooms, drained	
¼ cup catsup	
¼ teaspoon dried basil, crushed	
¼ teaspoon dried thyme, crushed	
1 cup crushed onion toast crackers	● For pastry, stir together crushed crackers, flour, and Parmesan cheese. Cut in butter or margarine and cream cheese till pieces are the size of small peas. Sprinkle *1 tablespoon* of the water over part of the mixture and gently toss with a fork. Repeat till all is moistened. Form dough into a ball.
1 cup all-purpose flour	
¼ cup grated Parmesan cheese	
6 tablespoons butter *or* margarine, softened	
1 3-ounce package cream cheese, softened	
4 to 5 tablespoons cold water	
1 beaten egg	● On a lightly floured surface, roll pastry to ⅛-inch thickness. Cut pastry into eighteen 4-inch circles, rerolling as necessary. Place *1 rounded tablespoon* of filling on *each* circle. Moisten edges with beaten egg. Fold pastry over filling to form a semicircle, then seal edges with the tines of a fork.
	● Place turnovers on a greased baking sheet. Brush with a little of the beaten egg. Bake in a 400° oven for 15 to 18 minutes or till golden brown. Serve warm. Makes 18.

Follow the old Boy Scout motto and "Be Prepared." Freeze the baked turnovers in foil and reheat them in the foil in a 375° oven for 10 to 12 minutes.

Maple-Syrup Meatballs

Pictured on the cover.

1	beaten egg
½	cup milk
½	cup cornbread stuffing mix
¼	cup finely chopped celery
1	teaspoon dry mustard
¾	pound ground fully cooked ham
½	pound ground pork

● In a large bowl combine egg and milk. Stir in stuffing mix, celery, mustard, and dash *pepper*. Let stand 3 minutes. Add ham and pork. Mix well. Shape into 1-inch meatballs. Place in a greased shallow baking pan. Bake in a 350° oven for 15 to 18 minutes or till done. Drain well.

Cook these meatballs ahead and freeze them for an impromptu party. Then reheat the frozen meatballs right in the sauce.

2	cups bias-sliced carrots *or* bite-size cauliflower flowerets
1	cup maple-flavored syrup
½	cup vinegar
2	teaspoons dry mustard
2	tablespoons cornstarch
2	tablespoons water
1	green pepper, cut into strips

● Meanwhile, in a medium saucepan cook carrots or cauliflower, covered, in a small amount of boiling water for 10 to 15 minutes or till tender. Drain well. In the same saucepan combine syrup, vinegar, and mustard. Combine cornstarch and water. Add carrots, cornstarch mixture, and green pepper to syrup mixture. Cook and stir till thickened and bubbly, then cook and stir 2 minutes more. Add meatballs. Heat through. Serve warm. Makes about 50.

In a saucepan combine syrup, vinegar, and dry mustard. Bring to boiling and add frozen meatballs. Cover and simmer for 8 to 10 minutes. At the same time, cook vegetables and combine cornstarch and water. Stir cooked vegetables, green pepper, and cornstarch mixture into syrup mixture. Cook and serve as directed at left.

Golden Glazed Chinese Ribs

Pictured on the cover.

2	pounds meaty pork spareribs *or* loin back ribs, sawed in half across the bones
1	tablespoon sugar
¼	teaspoon paprika
¼	teaspoon ground turmeric
⅛	teaspoon celery seed
	Dash dry mustard

● Cut ribs into single-rib portions. Rinse and pat dry with paper towels. In a small bowl combine sugar, paprika, turmeric, celery seed, and mustard. Rub ribs thoroughly with sugar mixture. Cover and let stand for 1 hour at room temperature or 4 to 6 hours in refrigerator. Place ribs, meaty side down, in a foil-lined large shallow roasting pan. Bake, uncovered, in a 450° oven for 30 minutes. Drain off fat. Turn meaty side up. Reduce heat to 350° and bake for 15 minutes more.

Ask your butcher to saw the ribs in half across the bones. It makes them easier to handle as appetizers.

½	cup water
¼	cup snipped dried apricots
2	tablespoons corn syrup
2	teaspoons vinegar
1	teaspoon lemon juice
¼	teaspoon ground ginger

● Meanwhile, in a saucepan combine water, apricots, corn syrup, vinegar, lemon juice, and ginger. Bring to boiling. Reduce heat. Cover and simmer for 5 minutes. Cool slightly. Pour mixture into a blender container or food processor bowl. Cover and process till smooth.

To make green onion brushes for a garnish, trim green onions at both ends. Cut thin 2-inch slits at one or both ends. Place in ice water to crisp and curl the ends.

	Lettuce leaves
	Green onion brushes (optional)

● Drain off fat. Brush ribs with apricot mixture. Bake 15 minutes more. Brush just before serving. Serve on a lettuce-lined platter. Garnish with green onion brushes, if desired. Makes 6 servings.

Cajun Occasion

Cajuns are former French-Canadians who resettled in the Louisiana bayous. They are a friendly and exuberant people who enjoy the simple pleasures of fellowship, festive music, and richly seasoned food. This easy menu not only gives you a taste of Cajun tradition, but also lets you spend most of your time where you belong—with your guests.

MENU
Wine Sparkler
Seafood Étouffée
Purchased French bread
Garden Salad Vinaigrette
Purchased pecan pie

MENU COUNTDOWN
1½ Hours Ahead:
Prepare dressing and assemble vegetables for Garden Salad Vinaigrette; cover and chill. Begin cooking Seafood Étouffée. Prepare Wine Sparkler.

5 Minutes Ahead:
Slice French bread. Remove pecan pie from refrigerator; bring to room temperature. Drizzle dressing over Garden Salad Vinaigrette; toss. Add shrimp to Seafood Étouffée; finish cooking.

Garden Salad Vinaigrette
(see recipe, page 37)

Seafood Étouffée
(see recipe, page 36)

Wine Sparkler
(see recipe, page 37)

Seafood Étouffée

Pictured on pages 34–35.

12 ounces fresh *or* frozen peeled and deveined shrimp ½ cup butter *or* margarine ½ cup all-purpose flour	● Thaw shrimp, if frozen. In a heavy large saucepan melt butter or margarine. Stir in the flour. Cook over medium-low heat, *stirring constantly*, for 20 to 30 minutes or till a dark reddish-brown roux is formed, as shown.
1 10-ounce can tomatoes and green chili peppers 1¾ cups water 2 carrots, cut into ¼-inch slices 1 stalk celery, cut into ½-inch slices ½ cup chopped onion ½ cup chopped green pepper 1 teaspoon dried basil, crushed ½ teaspoon salt ½ to ¾ teaspoon ground red pepper ¼ teaspoon black pepper	● Stir in the *undrained* tomatoes and green chili peppers, water, sliced carrots, sliced celery, chopped onion, chopped green pepper, dried basil, salt, ground red pepper, and black pepper. Bring the mixture to boiling, stirring frequently; reduce heat. Cover the saucepan and simmer about 25 minutes or till the vegetables are tender.
1 6-ounce can crab meat, drained, flaked, and cartilage removed 3 cups hot cooked rice	● Add shrimp and crab meat. Bring to boiling; reduce heat. Simmer, uncovered, for 1 to 3 minutes or till shrimp turns pink. Serve in bowls with a mound of rice atop each serving. Makes 6 servings.

An étouffée (A-too-FAY) is a type of stew in which shellfish is smothered in a seasoned vegetable mixture and served with rice. The dish begins with a roux (rhymes with stew), a cooked mixture of butter and flour. A Cajun will tell you to cook the roux till it turns the color of an old copper penny. Then you're sure the stew will have the rich look and taste that Cajun cooking is famous for.

Garden Salad Vinaigrette

Pictured on pages 34–35.

¼ cup white wine vinegar
2 tablespoons water
2 tablespoons salad oil
1½ teaspoons sugar
¾ teaspoon celery seed
¼ teaspoon dry mustard
¼ teaspoon salt
⅛ teaspoon ground red
    pepper

● For dressing, in a screw-top jar combine white wine vinegar, water, salad oil, sugar, celery seed, dry mustard, salt, and ground red pepper. Cover and shake well. (To store dressing, chill in the refrigerator.)

To keep the sliced avocados from turning brown, toss the slices with a little of the salad dressing before adding them to the salad.

1 small head Bibb lettuce,
    torn into pieces
1 small red onion, sliced
    and separated into rings
2 avocados, seeded,
    peeled, and sliced
1 cucumber, halved
    lengthwise and sliced
½ cup sliced radishes

● In a large bowl combine lettuce, onion, avocados, cucumber, and radishes. Shake the dressing well and pour over salad. Toss lightly to coat. Makes 6 servings.

Wine Sparkler

Pictured on pages 34–35.

1 1-liter bottle rosé wine
1 6-ounce can frozen pink
    lemonade concentrate,
    thawed
2 10-ounce bottles (2½
    cups) carbonated water,
    chilled
  Ice cubes
6 lemon slices

● In a pitcher combine the wine and the lemonade concentrate. If making ahead of time, cover and chill.

   Just before serving stir in the chilled carbonated water. Serve over ice cubes in glasses. Garnish with lemon slices. Makes 6 (10-ounce) servings.

Serve this light and tangy beverage with the meal or hand your guests a glass to enjoy before dinner. When they're down to the last few sips, slip into the kitchen and put the finishing touches on the étouffée.

Trim-a-Tree Party

Holidays, cookies, and children—you can't ask for a better party combination. Whether it's Christmas, Thanksgiving, or Valentine's Day, the kids will love making an ornament for a holiday tree (see tip, page 40), or decorating a Cookie Tree to fit the season. To keep it simple, bake the cookies ahead. Then, when the guests arrive, just set out the decorating supplies and let the artists go to work. (See recipes, pages 40 and 41.)

MENU
Make-an-Ornament Cookies *or*
Cookie Trees
Holiday Nog

Make-an-Ornament Cookies

Pictured on pages 38–39.

2¼ cups all-purpose flour 2 teaspoons baking powder ½ teaspoon ground nutmeg (optional)	● In a small mixing bowl stir together flour; baking powder; and if desired, nutmeg. Set flour mixture aside.
½ cup butter *or* margarine 1 cup sugar	● In a large mixer bowl beat butter or margarine with an electric mixer on medium speed till softened (about 30 seconds). Add sugar and beat till fluffy.
1 egg 2 tablespoons milk ½ teaspoon vanilla	● Add egg, milk, and vanilla, then beat well. Gradually add flour mixture and beat till well blended. Cover and chill dough about 1 hour.
	● Roll out dough, half at a time, on a lightly floured surface to about ¼-inch thickness. Cut into desired shapes with cookie cutters or knife, rerolling dough as necessary. Transfer cookies to ungreased cookie sheets. With a plastic drinking straw, make one hole at top of each cookie.
	● Bake in a 375° oven for 8 to 10 minutes or till cookies are light brown around edges. While cookies are hot, if necessary, reopen holes with a toothpick. Remove cookies from sheet to a wire rack, then cool completely.

Assorted decorations
(colored sugar,
small multicolored
decorative candies,
and/or crushed hard
candies)
Narrow ribbon
Assorted tinted creamy
white frostings* *(use a creamy white frosting mix)*
	● Put assorted decorations in individual small plastic bowls.
	    Tie a small piece of ribbon in the hole of each cookie for hanging.
	    Let guests decorate the cookies by attaching the decorations to the cookies with some frosting.
	    Let cookies stand about 30 minutes or till the frosting is slightly dry. Makes about 36 cookies.

MENU COUNTDOWN
1 day ahead:
Bake cookies and store in a covered container.
Several hours ahead:
For Make-an-Ornament Cookies, put decorative candies in small individual bowls. Make and cover frostings.
    For Cookie Trees, dilute food coloring with water.
    Prepare, cover, and chill Holiday Nog.
During the party:
Set out the cookies and decorations, frostings, or food coloring mixtures.
    Serve Holiday Nog while guests are decorating cookies.

While the cookies are drying, keep the kids busy making other ornaments for your holiday tree. They can string popcorn, make paper chains, or cut out paper tree ornaments.

Christmas isn't the only time to decorate a tree. During the rest of the year, get a full-looking bare branch and stand it up in a pail of sand. Then make turkey, egg, or heart ornaments and have a Thanksgiving, Easter, or Valentine tree.

Cookie Trees

Dough for Make-an-Ornament Cookies (*use recipe on opposite page*)

● Prepare cookie dough as directed, *except* omit the nutmeg. Cover and chill dough about 1 hour.

Meanwhile, cut a paper pattern according to directions at right.

● Roll out dough, half at a time, on a lightly floured surface to about ¼-inch thickness. With a sharp well-floured knife, cut dough into tree shapes using the paper pattern. With a toothpick, mark the *center* of each cookie. Transfer cookies to greased cookie sheets.

With the knife, slash *half* of the cookies from the top of cookies to the center. Slash the remaining half of the cookies from the bottom of the cookies to the center.

● Bake in a 375° oven for 8 to 10 minutes or till cookies are light brown around edges. While cookies are hot, cut a ¼- to ⅜-inch-wide slot along slash. (Slots need to be as wide as cookies are thick.) Cool cookies on cookie sheet for 1 minute. Remove cookies from sheet to a wire rack, then cool completely.

Desired food colorings
Water
Artist paintbrushes

● Dilute ¼ *teaspoon* of each desired food coloring in *1 tablespoon* water.

Give each guest a bottom-slotted and a top-slotted cookie. Using paintbrushes and diluted food coloring, let guests paint designs onto the cookies.

● Assemble trees, as shown at right. Makes about 8 trees.

To copy cookie tree, draw a 4x4½-inch rectangle. Divide it into ½-inch squares. Mark your grid exactly where the outline of the tree intersects each line on our grid. Connect marks. Cut out design.

When the cookies are dry, assemble the trees by slipping the bottom-slotted cookies into the top-slotted cookies to form three-dimensional trees. If necessary, trim slots to fit.

Holiday Nog

5½ **cups milk**
1 **package 4-serving-size** *instant* **French vanilla pudding mix**
2 **tablespoons sugar**
¼ **teaspoon peppermint extract**

● In a blender container combine about *half* of the milk, pudding mix, sugar, and peppermint extract, then cover and blend till smooth. Pour into a large pitcher. Stir in the remaining milk. Cover and chill till serving time.

Crushed striped peppermint candy
8 **striped peppermint candy sticks (optional)**

● To serve, stir and pour into glasses. Sprinkle with crushed candy. If desired, serve with peppermint sticks as stirrers. Makes 8 (6-ounce) servings.

Indian Curry Feast

In northern India, special occasions give rise to spreads such as this. One of the area's classic foods is korma, a dish in which meat is braised with yogurt or cream. Unlike some hot Indian dishes, *Beef Korma* and the other foods in this menu are gently but richly spiced.

Indians typically eat with their fingers, using bread to scoop up morsels of food. It's acceptable to use knives and forks, but purists claim the food won't taste as good.

MENU
Beef Korma
Indian Spiced Rice
Tomato-Apple Chutney
Spiced Meat Flatbread
Sautéed Cauliflower with
   Ginger
Cucumbers in Yogurt
Cool water or hot tea

MENU COUNTDOWN
6 Hours Ahead or Day Before:
Prepare Tomato-Apple Chutney; chill. Prepare Cucumbers in Yogurt; chill. Prepare Spiced Meat Flatbread; chill.
3 Hours Ahead:
Blend spice mixture and simmer meat for Beef Korma.

45 Minutes Ahead:
Cook Indian Spiced Rice. Begin cooking Sautéed Cauliflower with Ginger.
15 Minutes Ahead:
Reheat Spiced Meat Flatbread. Thicken Beef Korma with cream mixture. Finish Sautéed Cauliflower with Ginger.

Cucumbers in Yogurt
(see recipe, page 47)

Sautéed Cauliflower with Ginger *(see recipe, page 47)*

Spiced Meat Flatbread
(see recipe, page 46)

Beef Korma *(see recipe, page 44)*

Indian Spiced Rice *(see recipe, page 45)*

Tomato-Apple Chutney *(see recipe, page 45)*

Beef Korma

Pictured on pages 42–43.

1 tablespoon coriander seed 1 tablespoon cumin seed 1 teaspoon cardamom seed (without pods) 1 teaspoon crushed red pepper 6 whole cloves	● In a blender container combine coriander seed, cumin seed, cardamom seed, crushed red pepper, and whole cloves. Cover the blender container and grind the spices to a fine powder.
⅓ cup water ¼ cup slivered blanched almonds 8 cloves garlic 1 tablespoon coarsely chopped gingerroot 1½ teaspoons salt ½ teaspoon ground cinnamon	● Add ⅓ cup water, the slivered blanched almonds, garlic cloves, coarsely chopped gingerroot, salt, and ground cinnamon. Cover the blender container and blend till the mixture has a paste consistency.
2 pounds beef *or* lamb stew meat, cut into 1-inch cubes 1 tablespoon cooking oil	● In a 4-quart saucepan or Dutch oven brown *half* of the meat on all sides in 1 tablespoon hot oil; remove. Repeat with remaining meat, adding 1 tablespoon additional oil if needed; remove.
2 tablespoons cooking oil 2 medium onions, thinly sliced and separated into rings	● Heat 2 tablespoons oil in the saucepan; add onions. Cook and stir over medium-high heat for 8 to 10 minutes or till onions begin to brown. Reduce heat to medium. Add blended spice mixture; cook and stir 3 to 4 minutes more or till slightly browned.
½ cup water	● Add meat and ½ cup water to the saucepan. Cover and simmer for 1½ to 1¾ hours or till meat is tender; stir occasionally.
¾ cup whipping cream ½ cup plain yogurt 2 tablespoons all-purpose flour ¼ teaspoon garam marsala 2 tablespoons snipped coriander *or* parsley Indian Spiced Rice (see recipe, opposite) *or* hot cooked rice	● Stir together whipping cream, yogurt, flour, and garam masala. Stir mixture into Dutch oven; cook and stir till thickened and bubbly. Cook and stir 1 to 2 minutes more. Transfer to a serving bowl; sprinkle with coriander or parsley. Serve with Indian Spiced Rice or hot cooked rice. Makes 8 servings.

One of the classic recipes of northern India is the *korma*. Rich with yogurt, cream, and aromatic spices, it typically is served on special occasions. The name actually means "braise" and describes the method in which the blended spices in liquid penetrate the meat.

Indian Spiced Rice

Pictured on pages 42–43.

¼	cup sliced green onion
2	tablespoons butter *or* margarine

● In a saucepan cook green onion in butter or margarine till onion is tender but not brown.

1⅓	cups long grain rice
½	teaspoon salt
½	teaspoon garam marsala
⅛	teaspoon ground red pepper
1	small clove garlic, minced
2⅔	cups water

● Stir in rice, salt, garam masala, ground red pepper, and garlic. Cook and stir over medium heat for 1 minute.
   Add water. Bring to boiling; reduce heat. Cover and simmer for 15 minutes; do not lift lid. Remove saucepan from heat. Let stand, covered, for 10 minutes. Makes 8 servings.

An Indian meal rarely is eaten without rice. Not only does it soak up the liquids of the other dishes, rice acts as a buffer for spicier dishes in the meal. Serve saucy *Beef Korma* over part but not all of this delicately seasoned rice, leaving some rice to eat with the rest of the meal.

Tomato-Apple Chutney

Pictured on pages 42–43.

2	large ripe tomatoes, finely chopped (2 cups)
2	large cooking apples, finely chopped (2 cups)
1	cup packed brown sugar
¾	cup red wine vinegar
1	medium onion, finely chopped (½ cup)
½	cup water
¼	cup light raisins
½	teaspoon salt
¼	teaspoon ground red pepper
1	tablespoon mixed pickling spice
2	inches stick cinnamon, broken in half

● In a saucepan combine chopped tomatoes, chopped apples, brown sugar, red wine vinegar, chopped onion, water, raisins, salt, and ground red pepper. Tie pickling spice and stick cinnamon in several thicknesses of cheesecloth to make a bag. Add to tomato mixture. Bring to boiling; reduce heat. Simmer, uncovered, about 45 minutes or till mixture is thickened, stirring frequently.
   Remove and discard spice bag. Transfer chutney to a bowl. Cover and chill. Store in the refrigerator up to 4 weeks or freeze. Makes 2½ cups.

Excite and refresh your palate by taking intermittent bites of this tangy fruit mixture with spicier foods.
   To make it easier to remove the whole spices from the chutney after cooking, tie them together in a spice bag made from several layers of cheesecloth.

Spiced Meat Flatbread

Pictured on pages 42–43.

1¼ cups whole wheat flour
¾ cup all-purpose flour
2 tablespoons shortening
⅔ cup warm water
    (100° to 110°)

● In a mixing bowl combine whole wheat flour and all-purpose flour; cut in shortening till crumbly. Add *half* of the water all at once; mix in with a fork. Gradually mix in remaining water, 1 tablespoon at a time, till dough forms a ball and can be kneaded.

On a lightly floured surface, knead dough about 10 minutes or till smooth and elastic. Cover; let rest 15 minutes.

½ pound bulk Italian
    sausage
½ cup chopped onion
1 clove garlic, minced
1 teaspoon ground cumin
¼ teaspoon salt

● For filling, in a skillet cook sausage, onion, and garlic till meat is brown, stirring to break meat into small pieces; drain. Stir in cumin and salt. Remove from heat. Cool completely.

Flatten each portion of dough into a 4½-inch circle. Center 1 rounded tablespoon filling on each.

● Divide dough into 8 equal portions. On a lightly floured surface flatten one dough portion with your hand or roll out into a 4½-inch circle. Keep remaining dough covered. Place *1 rounded tablespoon* of filling in center of dough, as shown at top. Bring up edges of dough to enclose filling completely, as shown at center. Pinch to seal. Repeat with remaining portions of dough.

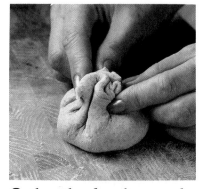

● Gently roll out each ball of dough into a 6-inch circle so filling spreads evenly inside dough, as shown at bottom. Dust occasionally with flour to prevent sticking to surface.

Gather the dough up and around the filling, pinching the seam to seal.

● Heat a griddle or skillet over medium heat about 2 minutes or till hot. Place one circle on griddle; cook about 2 minutes or till brown spots appear. Turn; cook 30 to 60 seconds more. Cool on a wire rack. Repeat with remaining. To store, wrap each in foil and refrigerate. (Or, wrap in moisture- and vaporproof wrap and freeze.) Makes 8 servings.

Note: To reheat, rewrap each flatbread in foil, if frozen. Warm refrigerated or frozen flatbread in a 300° oven about 15 minutes or till heated through.

Roll out again, this time into a 6-inch circle.

Sautéed Cauliflower with Ginger

Pictured on pages 42–43.

2 tablespoons cooking oil ½ teaspoon fennel seed	● In a 12-inch skillet heat oil over medium-high heat. Add fennel seed; heat and stir for 30 to 60 seconds or till seed turns brown. Remove from heat.
4 teaspoons grated gingerroot ½ teaspoon salt ¼ teaspoon turmeric ¼ teaspoon ground red pepper 1 large head cauliflower, broken into small flowerets (6 cups) ¼ cup water	● Stir the grated gingerroot, salt, turmeric, and ground red pepper into the oil and fennel seed in the skillet. Add cauliflower flowerets and water. Bring to boiling; reduce heat. Cover and cook for 10 to 12 minutes or till the cauliflower is crisp-tender, stirring occasionally.
½ cup coarsely chopped cashews 2 teaspoons lemon juice 2 tablespoons snipped parsley *or* coriander	● Increase heat to medium. Uncover and stir-fry 3 to 4 minutes or till liquid is evaporated. Stir in cashews and lemon juice. Sprinkle with parsley or coriander. Makes 8 servings.

Indian cooks use fresh gingerroot to accent the flavors of their vegetable dishes. You'll need about 2 inches of gingerroot that's ¾ inch in diameter for this recipe because each inch of the root will yield about 2 teaspoons grated.

Cucumbers in Yogurt

Pictured on pages 42–43.

2 medium cucumbers, peeled and finely shredded 1 8-ounce carton plain yogurt 2 tablespoons chopped fresh mint *or* snipped parsley ¼ teaspoon salt	● In a bowl combine the finely shredded cucumbers, plain yogurt, chopped mint or snipped parsley, and salt. Cover and chill in the refrigerator. Makes 8 servings.

Yogurt is included in almost every Indian meal, by itself, in a sauce, or with vegetables. Mixed with cool cucumbers and fresh mint, the yogurt in this side dish gives your taste buds a rest, especially if you are unaccustomed to so much flavor in one meal.

Index